Fount is an imprint of
HarperCollins *Religious*
Part of HarperCollins*Publishers*
77-85 Fulham Palace Road, London W6 8JB

First published in Great Britain
in 1993 by Fount Paperbacks
by arrangement with
Marshall Cavendish Books (A division of Marshall
Cavendish Partworks Limited)
119 Wardour Street, London W1V 3TD
Copyright © Marshall Cavendish Limited 1993
Concept, design and production by
Marshall Cavendish Books

Caroline Johnson asserts the moral right to be identified
as the author of this work

A catalogue record for this book is
available from the British Library

ISBN 0 00 627694-6

Printed in Hong Kong

ANGELS

Fount
An Imprint of HarperCollins*Publishers*

ANGELS

Angelos – 'messenger' – is the ancient Greek word from which
our modern 'angel' derives, and the prime function of angels
has always been to serve as messengers of the Almighty. These
spiritual beings appear in the holy literature of most of the
world's great religions, but in the Western world our ideas
about what angels are and how they look have been largely
formed by Christianity and the art of the Church.

In the Bible, angels are present in Paradise and at the Day of
Judgement, and they surround Christ at the most important
moments in his earthly existence. Angels are entrusted with
many duties. Some serve God by continually chanting His
praise. Some act as intermediaries between the Divinity and
mankind; they announce forthcoming events such as important
births, protect the righteous and they punish those who have
done wrong. Others serve man more directly as guardians and
comforters. Some angels are powerful beings in their own right
who can influence earthly events, turning the tide of battle,
stopping plagues and calming storms. While most angels are
wholly good, there are the legions of rebel angels who were
expelled from Heaven with Lucifer, God's most favoured angel,
whose pride caused his downfall.

Apart from Lucifer, the Bible names only three individual
angels – Michael, Gabriel and Raphael – although it states that
there are many different types. There has never been an
absolute consensus among theologians about the number and
nature of these heavenly creatures, but the main system of

classification can be found in a fifth-century work, *De Hierarchia Celesti*, which was later ascribed to Dionysius the Areopagite, a disciple of St. Paul. This book divides angels into nine choirs, grouped together in three hierarchies. The first hierarchy consists of Seraphim, Cherubim and Thrones, who remain closest to God, surrounding him in adoration and sustaining him. The second consists of Dominions (angels of mercy), Powers (who resist evil) and Virtues (angels of grace). The third comprises Principalities (who protect the earthly kingdoms), Archangels and Angels. The last two have the most direct communication with man.

Certain conventions for representing angels in art developed in accordance with Dionysius's system of codification. Seraphim and Cherubim were often shown as disembodied heads with wings, and as blue and red respectively. Thrones were sometimes shown as wheels with eyes and sometimes as angels holding thrones. Dominions might carry orbs or sceptres, Virtues might hold flowers such as lilies or roses, and Powers and the lower orders might be shown in armour or in more generalised garb. The thousands of angels who appear as accessories in Renaissance altarpieces – as musicians or companions of the Virgin and Saints – probably belong to the ninth and lowest choir.

In the Bible, angels are often mistaken for ordinary mortals, but in art these perennially youthful beings are generally shown with haloes and wings. Their wings may be plain or multi-coloured or even made of peacocks' feathers. Some are clearly based on those of large birds, like swans or eagles. Artists with scientific inclinations such as Leonardo may have considered the question of how the wings were attached, but they are never large enough to lift a body in flight. In early Byzantine representations angels are two-dimensional spirits on a flat background, but during the Renaissance they lost some of their ethereal quality and became three-dimensional creatures set in a believable space, with bodies as solid as those of humans. Their wardrobes also expanded to include not just the loose-fitting garments of the classical world but gloriously embroidered costumes: in some fifteenth-century Flemish altarpieces angels seem to be wearing full priestly regalia.

Theologians declared that since angels were pure spirit they were without gender, and most Renaissance paintings show them as effeminate males or androgynous beings. The naked child angels or *putti* are always male. However, later painters interpreted the question of gender more freely, and by the end of the nineteenth century many angels were depicted as unquestionably female.

Although Protestantism and science both conspired against the cult of angels, popular imagination has never relinquished its fascination with them. In our own predominantly secular age, religious belief in angels might have waned, but their decorative appeal flourishes unabated. They continue to adorn tombstones, greetings cards and wrapping paper centuries after the medieval scholars debated the question of how many legions of them would fit on a pinhead.

San Vitale, Ravenna

(c. 525 - 546)

———————◆●◆———————

ABRAHAM AND THE THREE ANGELS

This mosaic from the sixth-century Basilica of San Vitale
in the Italian town of Ravenna depicts an incident from
the Book of Genesis. While Abraham, one of the
patriarchs of the Hebrew nation, sits at the door of his
tent in the middle of the day, three men appear in front
of him. Abraham bows before them, fetches them water,
washes their feet and brings them bread and meat. The
visitors are angels, who prophesy that Abraham's wife
Sarah will bear a son, which she greets with laughter
since both she and her husband are elderly. However, she
later gives birth to Isaac in fulfilment of the prophecy.

The mosaic leaves no doubt that the mystery visitors in
loose fitting robes enjoying their meal are angels, as they
have haloes and a suggestion of wings. However, their
precise identity in the Scriptures has been subject to
much speculation. According to the Talmud, Sarah
recognised one of the three as the Archangel Michael,
and some cabala sources name the other two as Gabriel
and Raphael. Christian writers have seen their presence
as symbolic of the Trinity, and their announcement as a
prefiguration of the Annunciation.

Cimabue

(Active c. 1272 - 1302)

◆●◆

DETAIL FROM THE SANTA TRINITÀ MADONNA, C. 1280

These angels appear in Cimabue's large gabled altarpiece, or *Maestà*, which was painted for the high altar of the church of Santa Trinità in Florence. It shows the Madonna and Child seated on a splendidly ornate throne, with four prophets occupying a crypt-like space below and four angels ranged on either side. The whole composition is strictly symmetrical, the poses and garments of each angel being mirrored in its partner on the other side of the throne. The theme of the Virgin and Child enthroned, in which Mary is presented as a personification of the Church, is one that derives from early Eastern sources. Some of the earliest examples of this theme's occurrence in Italy appear in the mosaics at Ravenna's San Vitale basilica. Cimabue's angels are certainly Byzantine in appearance, resembling those seen on Eastern icons. But for all their rigidity, they are not without expression, and the gentle inclination of their heads, which echoes that of the Virgin, conveys a graceful melancholy. The details are also beautifully observed, from their shimmering wings to the curious, hooked-up bands they wear in their hair.

10

Giotto

(c. 1267 - 1337)

DETAIL FROM THE LAMENTATION, C. 1306

Some of the most expressive angels ever painted adorn the walls of the Arena Chapel in Padua. This tiny building houses one of the greatest treasures of early Renaissance art – Giotto's cycle of frescoes, which were painted for Enrico Degli Scrovegni. They depict the lives of the Virgin Mary's parents, of the Virgin herself and of Jesus Christ.

The Lamentation is set in a bare and rocky landscape. Christ's corpse is surrounded by mourners, including his mother, Mary Magdalene and St. John. While some express their suffering through gestures frozen in shock, others stand or sit still in attitudes of stoical resignation. But it is the angels hovering in the sky above who express the full anguish of the scene they have just witnessed: some weep into their hands; some cry out loud; some tear their hair out and others writhe and twist in torment. They are quite different creatures from the impassive Byzantine angels Cimabue had painted some twenty-five years earlier. Never before had heavenly beings been shown in such a dramatic display of sadness. It is as though the entire universe grieves.

Bernardo Daddi

(Active c. 1290 - 1349)

◆●◆

THE ANNUNCIATION, C. 1332

The Annunciation – the moment when the Angel Gabriel appeared to the Virgin Mary to tell her that she was to conceive a son to be named Jesus – is supposed to have taken place on 25 March, nine months before the Nativity. The subject is a central one in Christian art, and is frequently represented in altarpieces. The three elements usually present are the Virgin Mary herself, the Angel Gabriel (who often carries a lily or an olive branch) and a dove representing the Holy Spirit.

In this picture, however, there is an extra angel behind Gabriel. Although this is not the only instance of a painting depicting two adult angels visiting Mary to tell her the glad tidings, it is extremely rare. Various theories have been advanced to explain the identity of the mystery visitor. Some have suggested that he might be the Archangel Raphael; others that he could be the Virgin's guardian angel.

Bernardo Daddi, to whom this picture is attributed, was the leading Florentine painter in the generation after Giotto, and his refined figures in their delicate, detailed settings seem indebted to the earlier master.

French School

(c. 1395)

Diptychs are paintings in two hinged parts, which can be opened out like a book. They were often intended as portable altarpieces, and it is likely that this one belonged to Richard II. The King himself is shown on the left hand panel, kneeling in the company of King Edmund, Edward the Confessor and John the Evangelist. The right panel shows the Madonna and Child surrounded by several elegantly clad angels.

The precise meaning of the painting is obscure, but there are many allusions to the idea of kingship, with King Richard and the two other kings recalling the three Magi. Even the angels echo the theme of secular power; they all wear white hart brooches – the symbol adopted by Richard II – and sport collars of broomcods (the pods of the broom plant) similar to those worn by the King. One of them appears to be about to present Richard with the banner of St. George as the Christ Child leans forward to bless him.

Fra Angelico

(c. 1400 - 1455)

———————◆●◆———————

The mythology that has developed around the painter monk, Fra Angelico, is based largely on his early biographer Vasari's description of him as a pious and unworldly man who devoted his art to religion. The epithet 'Angelic', which was added to his name, also helped perpetuate the image of saintliness.

This jewel-like scene was commissioned by the Dominican monastery at Cortona. Early Renaissance paintings of the Annunciation often show Gabriel clad in white, floating on a cloud, but Fra Angelico has shown him rushing into the Virgin's loggia, resplendent in a red and gold robe. The artist usually painted his angels with multi-coloured wings, but here he has given Gabriel golden wings adorned with eyes. Gabriel does not hold the customary lily, but uses recognisably human hand gestures as he speaks to Mary. Their exchange (in Latin) is recorded in gold letters, and Mary's sentence 'Ecce Ancilla Domini' ('Behold the handmaid of the Lord') is written upside down so that it may be read easily by God above. In the background, Adam and Eve are being expelled from Paradise by an angel with a sword.

Fra Angelico

(c. 1400 - 1455)

◆●◆

DETAIL FROM THE LAST JUDGEMENT, C. 1432

In some Renaissance paintings Heaven is represented as a garden with angels who act as guides to the newly arrived souls. Fra Angelico's vision of salvation from his Last Judgement triptych is set in a flowery meadow, where angels dance in a circle with those who have been saved, while two of the elect enter the gates of Paradise. The angels have exquisitely gilded haloes and wings, and golden rays radiate from the heads of the blessed, some of whom are dressed in ecclesiastical garments. The Creator and saints preside over the central panel as graves are rent open and the dead rise from the earth to await their judgement. A grisly fate awaits the damned in the right panel, since this is the domain of the Devil and the tortures of Hell.

Fra Angelico's earliest training was as a miniaturist, and the brilliantly clear colours and perfectly painted details look as though they belong more to the intimate world of manuscript illumination than to the sphere of large-scale public art. It is hardly surprising that his biographer Vasari was inspired to describe his paintings as the work of angels.

Jan van Eyck

(c. 1390 - 1441)

◆●◆

THE ADORATION OF THE LAMB
DETAIL FROM THE GHENT ALTARPIECE, 1432

The Ghent Altarpiece stands in the Cathedral of St. Bavo in Belgium. Its two wings open out to reveal a series of inner panels depicting the heavenly and earthly spheres. The detail from the inside shown here portrays the Adoration of the Lamb as described in the Book of Revelation: 'After this I saw a huge number, impossible to count, of people from every nation, race, tribe and language; they were standing in front of the throne and in front of the Lamb, dressed in white robes and holding palms in their hands. They shouted aloud, "Victory to our God, who sits on the throne, and to the Lamb!" And all the angels who were standing in a circle around the throne, surrounding the elders and the four animals, prostrated themselves before the throne, and touched the ground with their foreheads, worshipping God...' A symbol of the sacrificed Christ, the Lamb stands on an altar, its blood flowing into a chalice. Angels kneel in prayer. One of them holds a crucifix and a crown of thorns – emblems of the Passion – and two others swing censers. In the foreground is the Fountain of Life, the source of salvation.

Rogier van der Weyden

(c. 1400 - 1464)

———◆●◆———

This side panel is from Flemish artist Rogier van der Weyden's vast altarpiece showing the Last Judgement, painted for the Hotel Dieu, a public hospital in the French town of Beaune. The Archangel Michael is leading the saved to the gates of Paradise, shown as a Gothic portal. The saved souls are naked as they have just risen from their graves. The nude figures were clothed in the early nineteenth century, but the clothes were removed during later restoration.

Angels have a prominent part to play in most paintings of the Last Judgement. They may be shown blowing trumpets to rouse the dead, shepherding souls to Heaven or driving them to Hell; some appear beside Christ in Majesty, bearing the instruments of the Passion. The Archangel Michael generally has the central role; in this altarpiece, he weighs the souls of the resurrected on a giant pair of scales. Although he was originally the guardian angel of the Hebrew nation, Michael was adopted by Christianity as a saint of the Church Militant, and is sometimes shown clad in a suit of armour with his sword unsheathed.

Master of Osma

(Active c. 1460)

◆●◆

ASSUMPTION OF THE VIRGIN, C. 1460

According to apocryphal texts from the third and fourth centuries, the body and soul of the Virgin Mary were reunited three days after her death and assumed into Heaven. The Assumption of the Virgin is a common theme in Gothic monumental sculpture and Renaissance and Baroque painting, but here it appears in a manuscript illumination in *The Breviary of the Bishop of Montoya*, housed in Burgo de Osma in Spain. As in most depictions of the event, angels have a central part in the drama. The white-clad Virgin, her hands joined in prayer, stands in mid-air resting her feet on a crescent moon, while angels carry her to her heavenly resting place. They have spectacular wings made from peacocks' feathers; the peacock was an ancient Christian symbol of immortality and the Resurrection. The music-making angels, who are usually present in scenes of the Assumption, have been banished to the margins of the illumination. The two top angels are placing a crown on Mary's head, an event often shown taking place after the Assumption, when Mary has attained her place by the side of Christ in Heaven.

Francesco Botticini

(1445 - 1496)

◆●◆

THE THREE ARCHANGELS AND TOBIAS, BEFORE 1470

According to a story in the Book of Tobit, Tobias encountered the Archangel Raphael as he was about to set out on a long journey to collect some money that was due to his blind father. At first, Tobias took him for an ordinary mortal; the wings that might have disclosed his divine origins were not a general feature of angels in biblical texts, although Botticini has painted them with loving care here.

During the long journey Tobias's companion helped him to acquire a wife and avoid being swallowed by a giant fish and destroyed by demon. However, it was not until they had returned safely that Raphael revealed his true identity. Raphael became an archetype of the guardian angel and is particularly associated with the protection of travellers and the young.

The text mentions only Raphael, but Botticini has added Archangel Michael (standing on the left, brandishing a sword) and Archangel Gabriel (standing on the right, bearing a lily). It is thought that Michael may be a likeness of Leonardo da Vinci, who would have been about eighteen when this picture was painted.

Verrochio and Leonardo

(1435 - 1488) and (1452 - 1519)

There is a long-established anecdote concerning the two angels who are holding Christ's garments in Andrea del Verrochio's painting, *The Baptism of Christ*. The young Leonardo was apprenticed to Verrochio at the time and, when he was twenty, his master entrusted him with the task of painting one of the angels in this altarpiece, which was destined for the monastic church of San Salvi, outside Florence. Vasari says that, after seeing Leonardo's angel, Verrochio never touched colour again, so ashamed was he of his apprentice's superior knowledge of the medium.

Whether or not the story had been elaborated by the time Vasari recorded it almost a century later, it does indeed seem that Verrochio concentrated on sculpture after 1472 – the date of this picture – relying on studio assistants to complete his oil paintings. Leonardo's angel, to the left of Verrochio's, radiates the graceful ideal of beauty that was to become his trademark.

Hugo van der Goes

(Active 1467 - 1482)

◆●◆

Scenes of the Nativity are often crowded with angels and this composition, which shows the Adoration of the Shepherds, is no exception. It forms the central panel of Hugo van der Goes's triptych painted for the wealthy Italian merchant, Tommaso Portinari.

The panel is a large one – about three metres wide – and the artist has included no less than fourteen angels in order to swell the ranks of characters that inhabit the vast space. The Virgin Mary, Joseph and the three shepherds kneel in front of the naked Christ Child, and they are joined by nine kneeling angels who help complete a circle around the newborn infant.

The angels look like solid but miniature versions of the humans. Just as there is a marked contrast in the refinement of the Virgin and the coarse rusticity of the shepherds, so there seems to be a kind of social hierarchy among the angels themselves: some wear the plain white or blue robes that are most commonly seen in Flemish depictions of angels, while others are resplendent in gloriously embroidered, coloured robes and multi-coloured wings.

Melozzo da Forlì

(1438 - 1494)

◆●◆

AN ANGEL MUSICIAN, C. 1480

Melozzo da Forlì, an Italian fresco painter from Forlì in the Romagna region and a pupil of Piero della Francesca, enjoyed the special patronage of Pope Sixtus IV. Among the highly prestigious commissions he received was one to redecorate the apse of the sixth-century basilica of Santi Apostoli in the Vatican. His fresco, which showed the Ascension of Christ, elicited great praise from all who saw it, but much of it rapidly deteriorated through age and damp.

Now only sixteen fragments remain, of which this depiction of an angel playing a lute is one. The other fragments also show angels – represented as beautiful youths – who are playing a variety of instruments, including a tambourine, a rebec, a mandola, a viol, a drum and a triangle.

They are the survivors of what appears to have been a large angelic orchestra of around twenty players, all celebrating the moment when Christ was taken up to Heaven in a cloud forty days after the Resurrection. The instruments chosen reflect the requirements of the Franciscan liturgy.

Master of the St. Lucy Legend

(Active c. 1480)

◆●◆

Three separate events in the life of the Virgin Mary – the
Immaculate Conception, the Assumption and the
Coronation – seem to have been merged into one in this
panel. Mary stands on a crescent moon surrounded by no
less than twenty angels. Six of the largest bear her up to
Heaven; three of them wear sumptuous ecclesiastical
garments complete with brocade and jewellery. It is
possible that they are the Archangels Michael, Gabriel
and Raphael. The smaller angels are more simply dressed
and play instruments of the period. Two angels by
Mary's head sing the beginning of *Ave Regina*. The choir
surrounding the Holy Trinity above plays quieter
instruments; the painter may have felt that softer
melodies were more appropriate for Heaven. By creating
such variety in the angels' appearance, the artist may
have meant to represent different ranks from the nine
choirs of traditional theology. It has also been suggested
that the colours of the angels' robes reflect the sounds of
the instruments they are playing. The panel is thought to
be by the Flemish artist who painted an altarpiece in
Bruges c. 1480, showing scenes from the life of St. Lucy.

Sandro Botticelli

(1445 - 1510)

——————◆●◆——————

THE ANNUNCIATION, 1489-90

In 1489 Botticelli was commissioned to paint this altarpiece for a family chapel. The mood is both intimate and contemplative: a gentle-looking Gabriel with abundant dark locks and sumptuous crimson and gold garments, carrying the familiar lily, kneels before Mary. She appears to shrink away from him, her eyes downcast. There is a remarkably subtle interaction between the two figures. Their bodies are separated but their hands almost meet across the void – Gabriel's raised in benediction and Mary's in defence. Words from St. Luke's Gospel are inscribed on the frame of the picture. Gabriel is announcing: 'The Holy Ghost shall come upon thee and the power of the Most High shall overshadow thee.' Mary's reply is: 'Behold the handmaid of the Lord: be it done to me according to thy word.'

Unlike earlier scenes of the Annunciation, which occur in rather vaguely defined settings, this one takes place indoors in the Virgin's chamber, where she has been interrupted reading at a lectern. Through an open doorway there are tantalising glimpses of a walled garden and a delicately painted riverscape.

Pietro Perugino

(c. 1445 - 1523)

DETAIL FROM THE VALLOMBROSA ALTARPIECE, C. 1500

The altarpiece on which these angels appear was painted for a monastery at Vallombrosa, in the hills to the south of Florence. Perugino, who probably taught Raphael, was renowned during his lifetime for his graceful and rather idealised figures, and the sweetness of his style complements his angelic subject matter.

In the centre of the altarpiece the Virgin is assumed into Heaven surrounded by a mandorla – an almond-shaped frame – of cherubim and seraphim. The Almighty, who is waiting above to welcome her to Paradise, is also enclosed in a circle of angels. Cherubim and seraphim were said to surround God in perpetual adoration. They are generally represented in art as heads without bodies but with one, two or three pairs of wings. Cherubim are usually blue and seraphim red but Perugino's angels do not have this supernatural colouring; with their chubby, babyish faces they are highly reminiscent of the infant *putti* that frolic through many a sacred Renaissance scene. Adult angel musicians with slightly wistful expressions serenade the Virgin, while others at her feet follow in flight.

Mathis Grunewald

(c. 1475 - 1528)

———————◆●◆———————

German artist Mathis Grunewald painted his masterpiece for the Anthonite hospice at Isenheim, in present day Alsace. The Anthonite order cared for the sick, particularly those with the Plague, so the altarpiece would have been meant to give spiritual comfort to the dying. It is actually a polyptych, combining several panels with wooden sculptures. Originally, the altarpiece contained two pairs of panels which were painted on both sides and could be opened and closed to make three different combinations of pictures. The panel showing a concert of angels faced one of the Virgin and Child, so that the angels appeared to be serenading them when the altar was first opened. Yet the image of the Virgin in prayer also looked out from the orchestra, so that Mary seemed to be addressing herself in the facing picture. The angelic musicians play their instruments in a bizarre Gothic chapel covered with scrolling plant tendrils. The angels are highly unusual: adults are mixed with curious fairy-like infants who have radiant haloes. To the left is the most fantastic creature of all – a feather-clad blue angel with an almost demonic countenance.

Raphael

(1483 - 1520)

In medieval art, angels tended to be portrayed as beautiful youths or stiff-limbed adults, with an air of heavenly remoteness that marked them out as being from an entirely different and more ethereal world than our own. But during the Renaissance, painters began to include infant angels in their pictures. They were modelled on the cheeky little assistants of Cupid, who acted as messengers of earthly rather than heavenly love, which were found in classical art and mythological painting. These impish creatures became known as *putti*. These two cherubs appear beneath the bank of clouds that support the figures of the Virgin and Child, St. Sixtus and St. Barbara in Raphael's Sistine Madonna, painted for the church of San Sisto in Piacenza. The child angels, with moth-like wings but without haloes, gaze upwards at the celestial vision above them. Their expressions and tousled hair give them a very human air, not unlike that of the Christ Child on whom they gaze in adoration.

Raphael

(1483 - 1520)

◆●◆

DETAIL OF THE LIBERATION OF ST. PETER, 1513-14

There are several episodes described in the Bible in which angels act as liberators. This central detail, which is taken from one of the rooms, or *stanze,* that Raphael painted in the Vatican, shows an angel on a mission of mercy to St. Peter.

In the Bible, the Acts of the Apostles describes how St. Peter was thrown into prison by King Herod during the period when the apostles were being persecuted. While he was asleep in his cell an angel appeared, telling him to arise. The angel led him past the guards and through the prison gates where he escaped without being noticed.

Raphael has shown the moment at which the heavenly visitor wakes the slumbering saint, and has made the angel's brilliant aura the sole source of light in the gloomy night scene. The next scene in the sequence shows the angel leading a rather bemused looking Peter by the hand past two sleeping guards.

The subject had a particular significance for Rome, as St. Peter was the city's patron saint. The painting has also been interpreted as an allegory of the deliverance of Italy from French invaders, who were expelled in 1512.

Caravaggio

(1571 - 1610)

According to the New Testament, Joseph was warned in a dream that King Herod was searching for the infant Jesus in order to kill him – which is why he took the child and Mary to Egypt, where they remained until the time of Herod's death.

The family's rest during the journey was a popular theme with artists in the sixteenth and seventeenth centuries. Caravaggio made the theme his own by including a semi-naked angel with strong erotic overtones. The angel is playing a violin to the Holy Family while Joseph holds a score, which contains a little lullaby in C major. In keeping with his penchant for naturalistic detail, Caravaggio has even included an extra violin string, which can be seen dangling from the angel's instrument.

The contrast between the alluring and youthful angel and the aged, clumsy Joseph is a poignant one. It is no coincidence that Caravaggio chose to depict the ground next to Joseph as barren and stony, while that by the sleeping Mary and her child is shown to be lush and highly fertile.

Pompeo Batoni

(1708 - 1787)

◆●◆

HAGAR IN THE DESERT, 1776

In its account of the life of Abraham, the Book of Genesis describes various instances of angelic intervention, including the announcement by three angels of the future birth of Isaac (see page 9) and the arrival of an angel to prevent Abraham from sacrificing him. The incident shown here relates to Abraham's first son, Ishmael, by Sarah's handmaiden, Hagar. When Sarah's son Isaac was born, she requested Ishmael's banishment. Abraham turned Hagar and Ishmael into the desert, equipped with only a skin of water and some bread. When the water ran out, Hagar placed her son under a bush to die, and sat down some distance away while the child wept. But God heard the boy wailing, and sent an angel, traditionally believed to be the Archangel Michael, who told Hagar to pick up the boy and hold him safe. He also showed Hagar a nearby well, where she filled the skin with water and gave her son a drink.

Batoni was the most successful painter in eighteenth-century Rome. In his highly polished depiction of the story the desert is green and shady, the well is a gushing fountain and Hagar a languid, neo-classical beauty.

William Blake

(1757 - 1827)

—◆●◆—

JACOB'S DREAM, C. 1805

When Blake was only eight years old he told his mother
that he had seen a tree starred with angels on Peckham
Rye in London. The angelic visions seem to have
persisted into adulthood, as the artist often claimed he
conversed with supernatural beings. Angels certainly
figure largely in his personal cosmology, writings and
art. Here they illustrate the story of Jacob's Dream, told
in the Book of Genesis.

As Jacob journeyed from Beersheba to Haran, night fell
and he lay down to sleep, resting his head on a stone for
a pillow. As he dreamed, he saw a ladder with angels of
God going up and coming down. Blake shows the
sleeping Jacob at the bottom of the composition, with a
spiral staircase, rather than a ladder, winding past a
starry sky into a radiant sunlit Heaven. Not all the
figures on the staircase have angels' wings; some appear
to be ordinary men and women. Two figures near the
bottom of the staircase – the angel carrying a basket of
bread and the woman carrying a pitcher – symbolise
God's gifts to mankind, which Blake described as 'The
Bread of Sweet Thought & the Wine of Delight'.

Dante Gabriel Rossetti

(1828 - 1882)

The Girlhood of the Virgin Mary, 1848-9

Rossetti's first important oil painting shows the young Virgin Mary as she is being educated by her mother. The artist's sister, the poet Christina Rossetti, modelled for the figure of the Virgin while his mother modelled for St. Anne. The child angel, itself a poignant symbol of innocence, is holding a vase containing a lily while Mary embroiders the flower onto a scarlet cloth. The flower is the traditional emblem of purity and is particularly associated with the Virgin, since it is often held by the Angel Gabriel in paintings of the Annunciation. Here, the presence of the young angel in Mary's chamber prefigures Gabriel's visit to the Virgin.

The books on which the vase stands are inscribed with the names of the virtues she is being taught. Their spines are inscribed with the Latin names for Faith, Hope, Charity, Fortitude, Temperance and Prudence. In the background, an oil lamp stands as an emblem of piety; the vine refers to the coming of Christ and the cross-shaped trellis foretells the crucifixion. The palm and thorn branch on the floor symbolise the seven sorrows and joys of the Virgin.

Evelyn de Morgan

(1855 - 1919)

◆●◆

THE ANGEL OF DEATH, 1890

There are angels of death in Jewish folklore, Islamic theology and Christian thought. But Evelyn de Morgan's depiction of the moment of death is an intensely personal interpretation filled with eroticism. As a young girl, the artist had written a poem on the subject, whose final two verses encapsulate the mood of this picture:

Oh Love in Glory
With Crowned brow
I feel thine arms
Around me now

Soft thy kisses
Warm thy breath
Vision of Love
Angel of Death

A black-clad angel stoops to gather the girl in his fatal embrace. Yet he is not a grim reaper; there is a tenderness in his gaze, and the beautiful Italianate landscape and golden glow of sunset bathe the scene in serenity.

Edward Burne-Jones

(1833 - 1898)

◆●◆

ANGELS OF CREATION, 1895

The Book of Genesis describes the Creation as having taken place over a period of six days. On the first day, light was divided from darkness; on the second day, there was a division of waters above and below the firmament; on the third, dry land and vegetation were created; on the fourth, God brought into being the Sun, Moon and stars; on the fifth, the birds and fish were created; and on the sixth was the creation of the animals, man and woman.

The subject of the Creation is one that is widely represented in stained-glass windows in Gothic churches but this window, based on a design by Burne-Jones, was installed in Manchester College, Oxford, by Morris & Company in 1895.

The whole window illustrates the Creation by presenting images which relate to the events of the six days within crystal balls held by six angels. Jenny Morris, William Morris's daughter, posed as a model for some of the angels, but others are of a more generalised type, reminiscent of those seen in paintings of the Italian Renaissance.

Arthur Hacker

(1858 - 1919)

THE CLOISTER OR THE WORLD, 1896

The theme of temptation is an ancient one in art, but
Arthur Hacker has transposed it into his own time in this
picture. While walking in the seclusion of her convent
garden, a young novice has suddenly been disturbed by
an enticing vision of the world outside in the shape of a
siren-like figure in a flowing robe. She has sunk to her
knees, clasping her rosary, and called out for divine aid.
An angel has appeared – clad in white and clutching a
lily stem, the ancient symbol of purity – who will
presumably help the nun triumph in her struggle with
worldly pleasures.

The angel and the siren form an interesting
counterpoint; the siren's diaphanous veil fans out behind
her like a pair of wings and the cupid who accompanies
her resembles the type of *putto* seen in Renaissance
altarpieces. The angel is clearly a woman and she looks
like a chaste version of the femme fatale she is
attempting to vanquish. The fact that the scene takes
place beneath an apple tree links it to the first temptation
of all, when Eve persuaded Adam to eat fruit from the
Tree of Knowledge.

W. A. Bouguereau

(1825 - 1905)

——————◆●◆——————

The French artist Bouguereau's painting is a reworking of the theme of the Virgin and Child enthroned, in which the Virgin is a personification of the Church.

The Mother and Child are surrounded by angels, who are dressed in white robes trimmed with gold; two of these figures are swinging censers while the others gaze on in adoration. Although the angels have beautiful, feathery wings, they wear golden tiaras rather than haloes, and their hairstyles are distinctly contemporary rather than ageless.

Quite feminine in appearance, these angels are very like the nymphs that appear in Bouguereau's allegorical and mythological works, although they are dressed with more propriety. This may have occurred because the nymphs and angels had a common origin: although he was an academic artist, Bouguereau was heavily influenced by the popular ephemeral images of his day, including postcards of both pious and erotic subjects. It is therefore hardly surprising that certain parallels have been drawn between his heavenly beings and the screen goddesses of early cinema.

Acknowledgements

———◆●◆———

The Bridgeman Art Library, London, supplied all the illustrations for this book with their customary efficiency. Special thanks are due to Harriet Bridgeman and Caroline Post for their encouragement and kind assistance.

p. 4 Staatliche Kunstsammlungen, Dresden; p. 9 Basilica of San Vitale, Ravenna, p. 11 Galleria degli Uffizi, Florence; p. 13 Cappella degli Scrovegni, Padua (Giraudon); p. 15 Musée du Louvre, Paris (Giraudon); p. 17 National Gallery, London; p. 19 Museo Diocesano, Cortona; p. 21 Museo di San Marco dell'Angelico, Florence; p. 23 Cathedral of St Bavo, Ghent (Giraudon); p. 25 Hotel Dieu, Beaune; p. 27 Osma-Soria Chapter House, Burgo de Osma; p. 29 Galleria degli Uffizi, Florence; p. 33 Galleria degli Uffizi, Florence; p. 35 Vatican Museums and Galleries, Rome; p. 37 Kress Collection, Washington D.C.; p. 39 Galleria degli Uffizi, Florence; p. 41 Galleria dell'Accademia, Florence; p. 43 Unterlinden Museum, Colmar; p. 45 Staatliche Kunstsammlungen, Dresden; p. 47 Vatican Museums and Galleries, Rome; p. 49 Palazzo Doria Pamphili, Rome; p. 51 Galleria Nazionale d'Arte Antica, Rome; p. 53 British Library, London; p. 55 Tate Gallery, London; p. 57 The De Morgan Foundation, London; p. 59 Manchester College, Oxford (photo: Ann S. Dean, Malvern); p. 61 Bradford Art Galleries and Museums; p. 63 Musée du Petit Palais, Paris (Giraudon).